Benched

Benched

*A TBI Survivor's Insight
into a TBI Recovery*

Ashley Welsh

Library of Congress Control Number:		2016915355
ISBN:	Hardcover	978-1-5245-4332-7
	Softcover	978-1-5245-4331-0
	eBook	978-1-5245-4330-3

Print information available on the last page.

Rev. date: 10/21/2016

To order additional copies of this book, contact:
Xlibris
1-888-795-4274 ˙
www.Xlibris.com
Orders@Xlibris.com
739464

Contents

Dedication

To the love of my life whose hand I held the tightest, you hold my heart KPW, and without your love, I could not have done this. To my three beautiful girls, Kaley, Madison and Brooklyn, you are the light of my life, and your love saw me through the hardest times. My therapy angels who caught my tears and sarcasm: JD, MK, Dr. K, and Dr. O. I thank my dear friends and family who wiped my tears, hugged away my fears, and prayed my pain away. And to the Lord above, whose presence I may not have always felt, but, I know he always had my back.

To the caretaker/loved one,

You are about to embark on a journey that peels back the layers of the trauma onion that your loved one is experiencing. And just as the layers are removed from an onion in the kitchen the pungency of the odor may bite your nostrils, and well up unexplainable tears. Allow this "onion to stir your emotional core As each layer of recovery is explained and explored on this horrific journey, I ask you to remove your apron and protective eyewear as you delve into the heart and soul of your loved one. Allow yourself to succumb to the understanding of exactly what your loved one is feeling, be stretched by this experience and open yourself to the plea of these words. Tear down your wall of protection and numbness so that your seed of hope and love may be saturated by these words and experiences.

To the trauma survivor,

First and foremost, you survived! I know that may not feel like a blessing and you may have remorse over that result, as did I, but, having survived, you now have a fighting chance, and fight you will. So put on your gloves, lace up, and get in the ring as you begin the rehab and recovery dance, weaving and bobbing emotions, situations and the pain that all try to land a sucker punch on your soul. Above all, know that you are not alone, you are being rallied by loved ones, and me, a stranger, but as you read, recognize that I am a sister in your suffering and may my words and experiences feed your soul and spirit, even though you may feel so lost and alone, I promise you, you are not! You may have to remind yourself daily that you are not alone.

Say What?

What you are about to read is quite simply *my* experience and by no means anyone else's story. This includes my personal feelings and thoughts. All of us come from different backgrounds and upbringings, which have molded our reactions, responses, and individual coping strategies. As my experience is not standard, it is not applicable to all. Quite simply, I am sharing my experiences and suggestions for supporting and rallying a loved one through a TBI (Traumatic Brain Injury) recovery. Although I cannot attest to any other form of health crisis, I imagine the feelings and thoughts would be similar at the very least.

My story culminated on October 31, 2013. During the prior seven years, I had experienced severe anxiety and panic with no medical explanation, other than a diagnosis of generalized anxiety disorder (which I didn't buy). I also experienced seeing blue dots in my vision. It seemed as though someone had taken my picture, and I felt the aftermath of the flash. I was also diagnosed with postpartum anxiety and depression because the anxiety coincided with the birth of my first daughter.

However, something in the pit of my being did not agree with this diagnosis either. But because I believed in the medical professionals, I succumbed to their diagnosis. Thus began the rough ride on the medication train, which included trying new, changing, increasing, and/or decreasing meds.

You would have thought that I was a walking pharmacy. Drugs could help one symptom, but they also might make things worse then other drugs to counter my reactions.

Fun, right? No, not at all. I still had the nagging feeling that I was not headed in the right direction, with my treatment or diagnosis. I took it upon myself to pursue the cause further, which led me to numerous endocrinologists and female health specialists. Again, the diagnosis ranged from PMS to low estrogen levels to possible hypoglycemia to possible thyroid issues. My head was spinning with the many differing possibilities, not to mention still being diagnosed with postpartum.

Who has postpartum, seven years after giving birth? That seemed completely absurd to me. And so, I felt as though I was sitting in the eye of a tornado watching all of the diagnoses swirling around me, slowly leveling my life. Something was not right! This led me back to my primary doctor, and I begged for more tests. She reluctantly conceded and suggested an MRI as I may have had a pituitary tumor. I happily took the script. For once, I felt I had been heard. As I left the doctor's office, I decided to run the errand on another day while my children were safely at school. As at this time, I only had a few hours before picking them up.

I will never forget that cold, damp, and dreary Halloween day as I raced to the scanning offices after dropping my youngest at preschool. I walked in, registered, and sipped my coffee in the waiting room. I was totally blasé as though this was a commonplace room and had no significance. This was a massive under appreciation on my part. After all, this is the room where others sat, just before learning they have cancer. This was pure ignorance on my part.

At last, my name was called. The tech instructed me to change into a hospital gown. So far, the procedures were typical. I was then escorted to the cold metal of the sliding table that enters the ring of judgment.

I followed directions very well, just as I always had before. Once I was notified that the test was done, I was escorted back to the changing room. I could now check that errand off of my task list.

As I walked out of the changing room, the tech met me at the door. Handing me a CD, he instructed me to see my doctor ASAP. What did that mean? I could feel my anxiety starting to ramp up "So you found something?" I asked.

Void of emotion, the tech quickly replied, "I can't tell you that, ma'am. Just take this back to your doctor as soon as you can."

Needless to say, what I thought was anxiety and panic before was now quickly overshadowed. I was consumed with fear and the dread of what this little silver disc was about to tell me. I remember calling my husband on my way home and telling him that I thought something was wrong. I explained that the technician gave no answers other than this was urgent, and I was to get to the doctor now!

Fortunately, my circle of life—my husband, home, and doctor—were all within walking distance of each other. As my tears mixed with the pouring rain, I managed to navigate my way home. I broke emotionally when I met my husband. What giant were we facing, and could we win? Could we handle it? What about our girls?

We rushed to my doctor, as she was expecting us and was given a heads up as to what she would be explaining. We were quickly taken to an exam room, once again we were left to our racing minds and consuming fears.

Suddenly, the doctor walked in, and I handed her the disc. I quickly asked what we were looking at. "Well, you have something called a cavernous hemangioma, which is quite sizeable. You need to see a neuroophthalmologist and a neurologist as quickly as you can."

I heard that word "quick" again. Why is everyone in such a rush now? Why did no one rush or care in the past seven years to help me? So immediately following my primary visit, while our girls were still in school. I was able to get into the opthamologist, where it was explained that this growth was pushing on my optic nerve.

A few days later, we were able to get into see the neurologist. This was when our world was shaken. I was informed that I had a growth in my brain that obviously didn't belong there. It was a malformation. Basically, it was a deformed blood vessel that showed evidence of hemorrhaging numerous times in the past twelve years.

I'm not sure why, but I had had an MRI in college and randomly kept the films, which we were able to use as a comparison to my current films. Shockingly, the older MRI showed that this malformation was non-existent at that time. This caused my surgeon to deduce that it had viciously erupted during the natural birth of our first daughter.

The timeline of symptoms now matched his theory. He explained that every time I felt a symptom, such as blurry vision, a tingling arm, or crazy bouts of anxiety, this growth was hemorrhaging and seeping deeper into my life. It was setting its roots onto my brain like little anchors setting up shop to wreak havoc in my life.

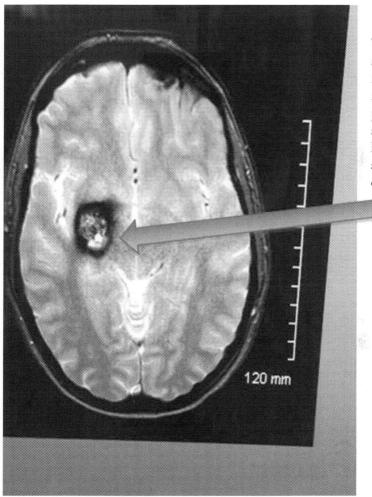

This white spot was the monster in my brain prior to surgery. This little devil was about the size of a golf ball.

Table Reservations

Ta-dah! Suddenly, the answers began to flow along side my tears. This "bubble" in my brain (as we referred to it when explaining to our children what was wrong with mommy) was pressing on my optic nerve. Therefore, it caused the blue dots in my vision. This little devil, the size of a golf ball, was located on my limbic center in the brain. This could cause my anxiety and panic.

And there you go, folks! I finally had an answer although not quite the one I expected. But nonetheless, it was an answer. This proved I wasn't crazy, and I was not making it all up. But yes, it was all in my head!

Contrary to popular belief, it is not an enjoyable experience being a human pincushion or a medication lab rat. I had a justified scientific reason for feelings of panic and constant nervousness. It also explained why all of the meds were not as effective as hoped. All I could think was *I told you so!* Seven Years of basically trial and error had led to this point.

Our next step was to see a neurosurgeon. *Wait, what ...? Surgery! On my brain?* Okay, things just got really real! What I originally treated as an errand quickly escalated on the list! The neuro surgeon was very concerned with what he saw and heard. The evidence had shown him that my little golf ball devil had hemorrhaged numerous times and was symptomatic! Therefore, we had to operate, which was not a typical course of treatment for these things. But because of the aforementioned, it needed to come out or it could kill me. Again, was this really happening?

Yes, I had wanted an answer, but not this one! At the end of our consultation, the doctor said, "Good work, you just gave yourself the best Christmas present." Had I, or was it a curse?

Yes, I learned that each person knows his or her body the best. If something seems wrong, it is worth checking out. This justification was bitter sweet. Finding an answer had opened up a whole new can of worms.

Surgery was needed. I was to be prepared for a year of fatigue and possible left-sided weakness. *Okay*, I thought, *I can handle that. After all, I had been fighting a seven-year battle, what was one more year? Fatigue seemed so much easier than constantly feeling like I was having a heart attack from the anxiety. Besides, who doesn't like to nap?*

So the scramble began. I needed to find someone to take care of our girls while I was down and out. Being the task-oriented woman that I am, I reached out to our church, where we found a young woman who seemed to be the perfect match to care for our girls. I also did all of the paperwork associated with my planned short-term absence. Looking at all of this as nothing more than mommy's job, I corresponded with the girls' schools, drafted letters of permission for family and caretakers to seek care for our girls with our health insurance, typed up schedules.

I was sorely mistaken in thinking this was preparedness for a short term sabbatical. I kick myself now for being so naive during this whole process. Not knowing that I was paving the road for my family during my extended absence, surgery had been scheduled for February 14, 2014. An earlier option was for January 17, but that was my younger brother's birthday. I didn't want to schedule it for that date. God forbid if something went wrong, I didn't want my brother to have that yearly reminder.

Apparently my knack for choosing dates is less than appropriate. As my luck would have it, a major snowstorm occurred prior to my scheduled dissection. So I kissed my children good-bye and left Valentine goodies and heartfelt cards that expressed my love for them in fear that something might happen. I wanted them to always know Mommy loved them dearly.

Dodging snow mounds and potholes, we made it to the hotel. I tried to relax during the stressful night before my D-Day. My parents had joined us as I was to be in the OR at five o'clock in the morning. We arrived early at the hospital, checked in, and I was prepped. I remember my mom meeting us at the hospital sobbing. I had to stay away from her as I was nervous enough without fueling my fear with her tears. Lying on the gurney, I signed one last release. To be honest, I guess I was signing my life away because I had no idea what the fine print relayed. Next, we all prayed around my bed before I kissed my husband good-bye. Looking back now, it literally was a good-bye, a farewell to the woman I'd been and life as we knew it.

When I woke up from surgery, my family learned that I had endured a stroke during my surgery. Unfortunately, I was not informed of my surgical complications as a means of "protection" by my family. However, and although I know they had loving intentions, I cannot imagine having been in their shoes, carrying the weight of such news about a loved one.

Upon reflection, it is very difficult to process the time I spent in the hospital and not knowing what occurred. I'm sure it was extremely daunting and difficult for my family to share such horrific news with me. Completely confused from my surgery, I was constantly tested with lights and hand squeezes. I also remember being fitted for hand and foot splints, which is mostly a precautionary method used in TBI to protect weak and overly tense muscles from contracting and to keep my toes from dropping down when I walked, to prevent me from tripping.

I should have known something was going on. But thank goodness I did not understand, because I never could have imagined that my complication was my new reality. I simply thought these interventions were typical procedures following brain surgery.

My family protected me from the predictions of any inabilities after my recovery. In hindsight, I learned that my prognosis was that I would probably never walk independently again or be able to speak. I was also informed I would probably lose my higher functioning skills, such as the ability to drive and the ability to care for my children independently. I am happy to inform you that I have defeated all of these odds.

As my luck would have had it, not only had I suffered one stroke as a result of the surgery. I had also suffered a subsequent stroke in my transport to inpatient rehab. It was explained that I needed to go there because it was where I was potentially regain the use and function of my left arm and leg.

The Pity Party

You have to be kidding me! This stuff doesn't happen to me! Well, unfortunately, it did. To say that I was shocked and angry is an understatement. Every profanity swirled through my head, and it was not because I had lost my filter during surgery. I quickly learned that the professionals tried to assign every action and emotion I exhibited to my stroke event and brain injury. Well, allow me to tell you, I was sure to correct every professional's thinking of this rationale, as I had every right to be emotional and angry, and therefore I would cry. Now granted, some brain injuries can cause emotional effects, however, this does not mean that individual is not experiencing legitimate emotional distress.

Please don't assume your loved one is gone forever if emotions are clouding their personality.! Your loved one is still in there even though they may be a little fuzzy, but please don't assume they are gone or hopeless! I had suffered a major sense of loss. I felt as though I had died, yet was alive to see it. Yes, I had a pity party, and your loved one may also. Allow it; don't try to stop it. If anything, try to understand it. Your loved one has suffered a major loss, and it's not fair! Let's be honest, you have suffered a loss as well. That loss will be faced every single day.

Obviously, a prolonged sense of pity and being swallowed by darkness is not healthy. Watch for severe depression. It is common and can occur with brain injuries. Your loved one may need the medical use of antidepressants. Yes, I had to try many different types and doses. Finally, one seemed to take the edge off and let a little light into my darkness, which had seemed impermeable.

Please understand this pity-party may happen on more than one occasion. The loss is bound to be remembered and mourned every single day. Who wouldn't feel depressed in this situation? But for the sake of your loved one, do not try to make them hide their sense of loss or minimize it.

Don't make your loved one pretend it doesn't hurt or shouldn't hurt as much. Don't put a time limit on how long the grief should last. Understand there may be daily mourning/grieving as tasks that were previously done with ease now present a major challenge or are impossible.

Do not make your loved one feel as though they are failing if they are not able to remain positive and wear a "perma-grin". This is not helping. It frustrates you as well as your loved one. They may feel they are not being heard or that their feelings are being minimized and disregarded. I would get so angry at those who would tell me, "Smile, and just be positive." I was positive, positive that this sucked, and I could not get out of it fast enough. I felt as though there was an unexpressed expectation for me to be *bulletproof* or a *superhero*, which I simply was not. Afterall, I am only human.

Numerous individuals made the same and most discouraging comment, "It's only a hand." Well, no, it was much more than that. That hand once held all my dreams and hopes. Now it held those aspirations captive. Angry when I heard that comment, I would ask the individual to go through just one day using only one hand and see how unbearable it was. Everyday tasks were no longer simple. Buttoning pants, putting lotion on my hands, doing my hair, making sandwiches, and folding laundry took more time. It seemed as though my feelings and pain were being minimized and overlooked. Granted, I knew deep down that none of these comments were made in spite, but rather out of well-meaning intentions and love. However, my emotional fragility only heard ignorance and condemnation.

One of the most hurtful comments was made when I tried to convey my frustration of not being where I wanted to be in my healing process. "Obviously, you aren't where you want to be because you are still complaining!" Really? If all you can see is your loved one's complaining, take a step back and breathe. You really are not trying to empathize with his or her pain. Bat are rather judging it.

My emotional pain was more than anyone could grasp. Sitting on my front porch in our busy little town, I watched walkers as they passed by and wondered if my life could ever go on like theirs. *Would I be able to walk briskly, accomplish everyday errands, and chase my kids like the moms I had witnessed? Could I pick up the mail or the dry cleaning?"* As I saw other moms lift their children into and out of their car seats, I thought, *Could I ever do that again? Could I ever put my daughter's hair up for dance class?*

I was consumed with jealousy and fear just from sitting on my porch. Imagine what stirred within me when I actually went out into society. I had many dark moments in which I really needed a hug and to hear that I would be okay. The fear of this being my future was too much to bear at times.

I cried a lot due to the internal pain that shattered my spirit. But I also cried because I could not make those around me understand where I was coming from and why it hurt so much. I felt as though those around me were treating me differently. Although this stroke was by no means my fault, it seemed as though I was bearing the punishment. It seemed as though I was wrongfully imprisoned for a crime I did not commit. My tears lessened for a bit. But once I neared my two-year mark of recovery, the tears began to flow more— unstoppable geysers of pain and remorse. As the battle fatigue grew and my frustration swelled, I never imagined spending my thirties fighting a geriatric condition.

In a close relationship, each individual is bound to end up frustrated and angry as neither party is able to convince the other of their argument or the intensity of emotions. The best medicine I can offer is to embrace your loved one and allow that person to share his or her pain with you, but don't try to fix it because you can't.

If, for some reason, you are shaking your head or fist in disagreement, I kindly ask that you put the book down. Quite simply, you may not be in the place or frame of mind to grasp or understand the depth of these words and that's okay. As stated before, these are my experiences and thoughts. These may or may not coincide with those of your loved one.

My loss of ability and identity were very traumatic, and I had to navigate them daily. The realization of the loss I would be facing caused me to question: *Who was the real me deep inside?* My value was no longer determined by my actions and abilities as these were no longer possible. I was much slower and not as productive; my fast-paced lifestyle had come to a screeching halt.

This is a very difficult question to ask oneself. It is also a long and hard learning process to go through, whether thrust into this situation or not. Such questions require insight from friends and family as to what traits or characteristics you admire in your loved one. Simply saying, "You are still the same person," suits no value.

Your loved one may ask, "Who am I?" or "What do you treasure most about me?" He/she is actually asking what characteristics/traits are valuable or recognizable. What do you treasure most about them?

So really, who is that person you say is the same? This road to self-discovery can be very painful as this person may be asked to let go of the identity they once held so dear. To me, it felt as though I were being asked to mutate my DNA. When I was forced to modify what was so deeply engrained in my being, I faced much internal resistance. Although you may be able to teach old dogs new tricks, it doesn't mean they like it. After all, the woman I had been for the past thirty-five years was completely different. Now I had to practice life differently.

Unfortunately, the inability to complete simple everyday tasks was magnified. As a mother, I was fearful *I would never do my girls' hair again—or my hair for that matter. Would I be able to fold laundry or do the* crafts I had so enjoyed doing? All of these tasks and more required two hands. I began to use a lot of clips and headbands for my girls' hair. No, they would not be on the cover of *Vogue* for trendy hairstyles. However, I was reclaiming what once was mine and what would be mine again. I was determined I was going to fight!

These tasks may seem like petty abilities to some. But from a mother's heart, these were parts of my identity and family contribution. Hence another challenge. I really had a difficult time finding my value again. I had always been task oriented, which until now, had defined me. Relying on others for my value was difficult. When I wasn't feeling my value to them, I felt no value at all. Some days, it thrust me into a pit of despair and disgust with myself.

This sense of having lost my identity was a huge challenge for me; it may be for your loved one as well. Prior to my surgery/stroke, I was the matriarch of the house. I did all the cooking, cleaning, and childcare/grooming. I kept the house in flow. Now, my ability to do such things had been severely hindered by the paralysis of my left hand and arm as well as the weakness in my left leg. Now, instead of the matriarch in the current, I was the undertow pulling everyone down.

When I finally came home from inpatient rehab, I was met with major struggles in trying to find my place back in my family. The position I once had held was no longer available to me. I no longer had the ability to hold or maintain that position.

My inpatient rehab stint had been the baptism of me in my new self- realization. Unfortunately, I had been severely degraded in rehab, which contributed to my lack of esteem and self-worth. During my stint in inpatient rehab, I had experienced some major emotional damage as I was faced with these insurmountable challenges. My cold and sterile room felt more like a jail cell than a facility to foster healing.

I was no longer able go to the bathroom by myself. When my bowel movements had to be verified by staff, I asked, "Seriously?" I had to be showered by others. To say that modesty was out the window would be an understatement, and this was coming from a woman who had three vaginal child births.

I had to ask to have my food cut up. I had to be dressed by others, sometimes male technicians. In this process, I no longer felt like a human, but more like a specimen, when I heard, "Oh, she's crying again. Let's start her on antidepressants." Show me someone who wouldn't cry facing such an impossible reality.

Allow me to encourage you to be an active participant in your loved one's stint in rehab if it is part of the recovery. Be aware of the treatment and care the patient is receiving and the medications being administered. At one point, we had a family meeting with the doctors in my inpatient rehab stay to discuss why I was on so many medications. Quite honestly, the doctors did not seem to know the answer.

One of the biggest challenges for me came in the days further out from the onset of this insurmountable challenge. When I was in the hospital, the gravity and immediacy of the situation grabbed many people's attention. Therefore, I had much support and visits. However, in the days to come, I went home and realized the challenge had begun.

My friends and support system were few and far between. Because I was no longer in the hospital, I felt others saw this as not as hard or important or that I must be okay because I was home, but it was very difficult. In the days after my two-year anniversary, I was alone and sobbing. Literally, I had no one to turn to. Yes, I had my family, but they were burned out too!

I had to be very cautious about who I reached out to. Some friends' loving words seemed to overlook the gravity of my situation. Others simply blamed my tears on the wrong dose or brand of antidepressant. I had to protect myself from condemnation and judgment as I felt enough of this internally.

It was so important to protect myself from reaching out to those who simply did not "get it" or those who would mutter hurtful compassion, such as, "Maybe you should go to counseling?" Others might ask, "What are the doctors doing for your depression?" or "Are you on medication?"

Yes, as a matter of fact, I was on medication. But taking a pill did not simply make the depression or the pain disappear although I wish it would have. I felt as though I was suffocating when the dark days creeped in. I had nowhere to turn. I called friends from years past just to hear another voice to help talk me through this mounting darkness.

No one understood the amount of energy it took to wake up every day and fight for two years straight. Instead, I felt the constant criticism to be a superhero. However, I simply could not manifest the strength from some crevice in me. I should have been done crying by now and just accepted my state. Never mind any dreams or hopes I had had for my life. Granted there were no right words to say. I know those trying to help were doing just that. They were trying, but it wasn't what I needed.

Looking for the Lighthouse

You may not understand what your loved one is going through, so allow me to shed some light on the internal suffering as I felt it.

It was as though I was sailing on peaceful seas when an unpredictable squall hit my boat. Suddenly it took on water in the middle of the ocean. Desperately, I looked around, but couldn't find the lighthouse or anything to point to safety or the familiarity of home. Nothing indicated the promise of ever standing on dry land again.

I fought hard to keep my head above water, but my body started to ache from the fight and fatigue. I still saw no beacon of light. But if I stopped treading, I would sink.

I tried to recite the Sunday school verses through my head: "Be strong and courageous. Do not be afraid or terrified because the Lord your God goes with you; He will never leave or forsake you" (Deuteronomy 31:6 NIV)

"For everyone that asks, receives; and he that seeks, finds, and to him that knocks, it shall be opened" (Matthew 7:8 NIV).

At this point, I was knocking so hard that my knuckles bled. Finally, I saw a lighthouse and had hopes of dry land. However, it was a light on a distant boat that was traveling in the opposite direction. My fear and uncertainty drowned out any hope. The hope I held for a nanosecond had quickly sunk to the sea floor as well as my heart.

So I swam aimlessly with hopes that I would make it to shore someday, but still no promise. I screamed, but no one heard me. Instead, the other passengers on the boat told me to stop screaming because I was too loud.

I was wasting my breath and scaring the fish. What was I supposed to do? Just lie back and float while I pretend that I never want to stand firmly on the ground again? You're right, it's so fun being soaking wet, cold, and scared, but turn those emotions off as they won't do any good. I reached out for anything to grab onto, but what I thought was debris floating by was only shadows and false hope in the night. I screamed out for God, but he's taken an extended lunch break with headphones on.

My screams barely made it past my lips because I quickly felt as though I wasn't being heard. Instead, I was destined to doggy paddle for eternity and never get tired.

For the love of God, please do not treat your loved one as if he or she is stupid. That person you care for is still there even if he or she is not able to perform the way everyone is used to.

Yes, I had had an injury to the brain, but please keep in mind, this was not by any means a choice. Your loved one is in there, maybe under some layers of fog and confusion, but your loved one is still in there. Obviously, there may be some cognitive results. Again, he/she did not choose this, so please do not patronize and treat them as if they are dumb or less than respectable. The emotions and feelings are very much real. Us survivors know when we are being talked down to, or are being treated as a child.

Anger surged when people would ask me, "Do you understand?" Did they think because of this injury that I was incapable of understanding and conceptualizing the conversation? This does not go to say, that others may not experience cognitive impairments causing them not to understand, but this does not remove their right to be treated respectfully and like a human. Granted, my reaction to questions may not have been as quick as some would have liked.

However, when you fell off of your bike and scraped your knee as a child, did you jump back up, brush away the dirt and blood, and hop back on the seat and start peddling? Well, think of your loved one in that visual. After falling off of the bike, a few bruises appeared. Don't expect anyone to jump up enthusiastically, get on the bike, and ride full speed again while pretending as though nothing has happened.

If you couldn't do it, don't expect your loved one to do so with a legitimate injury that was out of his or her control. The circuit board to your loved one's entire physical being has fallen off the bike and has some scrapes and grass stains to show for it. No bandage is big enough or colorful enough to take away this pain and make it all better.

Over time, I also encourage you to allow your loved one to assert some independence, safely of course. For example, I refused to let others fold my laundry, do my dishes, or even help me get dressed. I will be the first to admit these executions were not pretty spectacles. However, the point was that these were *my* tasks and I was determined to do them. Of course, I was frustrated as hell because I could not do things like I used to, but I would not give in.

I was not about to lose my independence. I had lost enough already. This also meant doing things completely out of my comfort zone. For example, we went on a family vacation and the kids decided they wanted to climb a ten-story lighthouse. Not my finest moment, but I did it because I was not going to be left behind!

Independence also meant going to indoor play spaces with my children. Although I could not keep up with them or climb the obstacles, I again refused to be benched. I was going to take my place back on my team! Please, don't assume that

I did these things without pain. Emotionally, I was dying a little bit inside every time, but I had to swallow that pain to keep trudging forward. It would all come out in tears later anyway, and that was okay.

So that was how I processed my hemotional pain It's not as though I could run to burn off steam, so crying was my only productive outlet. I cried a lot by myself, especially after all my children were off to school. I would walk around my house screaming and sobbing without judgement or vocabulary censoring. I could be me to feel and express all of the pain churning inside.

Beliefs Challenged

I have to admit that one of the hardest challenges for me was the testing of my faith. I had grown up in the Christian church with a Christian family. My faith was an integral part of who I was. I had traveled the world spreading the good news while serving on numerous mission trips and leading Bible studies. At this point in my life, I felt like a giant hypocrite.

Yes, I still believe in God, but I had a difficult time believing He would heal me, or that he was there for me. At this point in my life, however, I realized that I didn't necessarily have faith. I had God but not the faith. This was a difficult epiphany for me. It challenged all that was so deeply engrained in my heart and spirit. Trust me, I had words with God—many of which were not that nice. However, as emotions were God given, I had a right to express them to Him.

Over time, I learned how hard it was to remain faithful. We are not naturally wired to believe what we do not see. After all, how often do you hear, "I'll believe it when I see it?" I have to be honest. Believing the unseen takes real work. Sometimes, I did not have the energy for more work as everything seemed like work at this point. This is where the faith and support of friends became imperative to me. They held me up when my own two legs could not support the weight I was fcarrying.

Fold Up the Box

I encourage you to do one another favor for your loved one: Never set limits on what is possible.

During a physical therapy (PT) visit, I asked the therapist if she thought I would ever be able to walk without an assistive device (cane, walker, or electric stimulation). She simply replied, "I don't think so." That quickly took the wind out of my sails.

It also reminds me of an incident during my stay in rehab. A nurse had approached me in the patient dining room. Obviously, I was emotional. I can't imagine why. I was no longer eating in my family dining room with my three girls and husband every night. Instead, I was eating in what appeared to be a nursing home's parking lot for wheelchairs. The walls were adorned with cheesy paintings and vases with obviously fake silk flowers. The intent was to bring much needed cheer to the patients in the facility.

One afternoon, immediately after my husband had visited with my girls, I was wheeled to dinner. I was extremely tearful at their departure, but more so to be remaining in the nursing home. As my left arm dangled on the side of my wheel chair, my tears flowed like the Hoover Dam. I was approached by a staff nurse. Obviously, she felt compelled to cheer me up and give me her two cents. She voiced some very consoling words among unsolicited words. She not only stated that I was suffering from PTSD, but she added that I would never get the use of my arm or hand back!

Didn't she realize that even if all that were true, she wasn't doing me any favors by calling it out? It surely didn't make me feel better! Apparently, compassion was not part of her employee handbook or training. This harsh insight was not helpful by any means. Actually, it made the tears fall harder and the parking lot that much more repulsive and nauseating.

The orange fluorescent lights of the medical facility quickly grew darker and darker. No words of encouragement could drown out the *never* that had been singed on my brain and my heart. Little did she know; she just said that to the wrong person. Her "You will never" gave me that much more fuel to fight like hell and prove her wrong.

One of the biggest issues in the medical world is the tendency to put TBI and stroke recovery in a box labeled, "This is how it happens" or "This is how recovery has to happen." Yes, trends in recovery show how muscles and nerves tend to return. For example, my arm was to return proximal to distal (shoulder to elbow, wrist to hand with fingers being last). Well, I was the out-of-the-box patient.

I had wrist movement, although weak, before I had shoulder and elbow movement. Next, I was able to squeeze my hand. This was yet another challenge for those involved in my care who thought, *This wasn't the way recovery is supposed to happen.*

Says who? Is there an instruction manual for stroke/TBI? If so, I surely could have used one. Is the recovery the same for everyone? Wasn't some return, no matter what the sequence, better than none at all? My return still had to be strengthened and finessed, but I would think having something to work with provides for a better outcome than having nothing at all.

Do not place limits on the limitless. The brain is an amazing entity. It doesn't like being "broken" as my children and I referred to it. During my recovery I began to see a chiropractic neurologist who explained to me that my brain was listening to what I was saying about it. I rarely had kind words about my brain; in fact, we had a very tumultuous relationship. My brain and I were not friends.

The Rehab Dance

I call the road in rehab "the rehab dance" for a very simple reason. You may have to try different recovery partners until you find the one that makes your loved one dance the best— physically, mentally, and emotionally.

First, I would recommend finding a PT and an occupational therapist (OT) that not only are invested in your loved one's recovery, but whose personalities are a good combination with your loved one. You would be amazed at the number of therapists who take their role as only a job. Unfortunately, they may consider your loved one as just a file or co-pay. Many therapists are not invested in the quality of the outcome. After all, they are not the ones who will live with altered function or movement.

I found these traits in my dance partner to be very beneficial. During my recovery, I would become emotional during my therapies. This was due to the "battle fatigue" of stroke recovery and questioning the extent of my recovery and function. My therapists were very insightful and encouraging during my tearful recovery. Mixing it up with some humor and sarcasm proved beneficial for me as well. Let's just say, I was not the typical docile patient. As I was about the same age as my therapist, which allowed us to act our age.

Again, from my experience, I would offer one suggestion to the patient's loved one: Try everything possible as part of your loved one's treatment menu. Obviously, PT and OT are standards in this type of recovery. However, the standards are not the only means to recovery. I found that using out-of-the-box approaches also deemed valuable.

For example, I used acupuncture even though I was told it wouldn't help me. On my first visit, I was wheeled in. A few weeks later, I walked in with a cane. The point is, I walked and had some control of my ankle that had bad foot drop on my left leg. Typically, that is managed by wearing a foot brace. This was another example in which I stubbornly refused; I was not going to give in. Stroke was not going to win! I was going to walk without a brace!

I also had an approximate two-inch subluxation or separation in my left shoulder that caused my arm to dangle like an arm on a string puppet. Acupuncture helped to put my shoulder back in its place.

I also decided to go to a chiropractic-neurologist. Again, and by no means, was this a typical mode of treatment. I was educated that brain balance had to be reestablished in order to regain function.

I was floored at the changes that I had made during this treatment method. The doctor went right to work on the root of the problem—my brain. By using neuro exercises, which included many visual training exercises, my vision or lack thereof on my left side was a contributing factor to my physical condition.

After a few short months of religiously completing my exercises, my arm no longer curled up when I walked. Now, it hung straight and didn't dangle. It was beginning to look like a typical arm. And I no longer felt as though I constantly resembled an orangutan.

The vision on my left side started to return. Originally, I had a significant area of blindness on my left side. I learned that my brain did not depend on the duration of these exercises, but was "dose dependent" and thrived on repetition. I was cleared to return to driving. Although my confidence in something that previously came so easily was now fear inducing. The point was I could now drive my children to school, go to the grocery store, and drive myself to my appointments. I no longer had to rely on others. Score! One more point for me; one less point for the stroke.

Although I could drive now, it was not as before. I had to drive with a spinner knob with wireless turn signals and horn, since I could not use my left arm for these functions. Still, it was yet another ability that I so desperately wanted back!

During my treatment, my walk became smoother, and my balance improved. I was also able to wean off of the medicines that relaxed my tone (also known as muscle tightness or spasticity) as my brain was now learning to do it on its own. Yet another point for me!

So, out-of-the-box, yes! Worth it? Absolutely, without a doubt! Again, please do not put limits on the limitless! Be open to anything and everything that may help. It's amazing what desperation for healing can do to open doors worth exploring and within reason.

Another mode of rehab that I recommend is prayer for the individual and family. The laying on of hands and requesting prayer from churches and friends was very powerful for me. I had hoped and begged for a miraculous healing, but I was not the lucky recipient. Still, that does not mean it doesn't happen or that prayer is not beneficial. Although it cannot be proven, I am convinced that prayer played its part in my unpredictable and nontypical recovery as well as the healing of my arm and hand that were once deemed lifeless.

During this horrible chapter of my life, a few things really contributed to my spirits. One was the introduction of Stephen's Ministries. Most often, this ministry is sponsored by a local church. Basically, this ministry partners a church member with a mentor who walks with you during tragedy.

I called Stephen's Ministries on the day I hit my absolute lowest and wanted to die. I couldn't take it. How could I live my life this way? My mentor and I met once a week. Basically, I would check-in with her and connect on a friendship level.

Let's be honest, at least for me. Some of my friends and family were burnt out by me and my problem. It was too big for them to handle, so they pulled away. And so another loss compounded by my situation. I needed someone who wasn't going to bail out. For me, that was my Stephen's mentor. She always had my back, and we became great friends through this process. She prayed for me in the times I could not. I listened to spirit lifting music and watched television shows that did the same.

The Journey of Recovery

Unfortunately for many, the road to recovery is not a quick trip and often feels as an open-ended journey. At least it did for me. With a lot of hard, grueling work and therapy, I rarely saw results. For me, it was the one job I had, and I could not immediately see the fruits of my labor.

Unfortunately, it took months to see positive changes. That did not mean internal changes were not happening. My chiropractic-neurologist referred to this as trying to watch grass grow in the winter. It was happening underneath, but it couldn't be seen from the surface. This was an especially hard time for me and I needed to surround myself with positive and encouraging people. I highly recommend that anyone who is in a TBI situation to be very cautious as to who is in your inner circle and protect the epicenter.

During my recovery, I lost many friends that I thought were close to me. Apparently, my challenge was too challenging for them. I hoped those friends were never faced with insurmountable challenges that beg them to lean on others for life-giving breath and support. Try to surround yourself with those who encourage you. At times, you may need to rely on others for hope, as I needed to rely on others to hold the faith for me too.

The best way to describe the journey of recovery is walking from New Jersey across country to California wearing a blindfold. However, as you are walking, you have no idea where you are or how much longer the trek will be or what scenery you are missing. Still, you keep on walking and thinking that someday you will reach California. How or when that may be is unknown. Sometimes, it felt like an aimless and endless trek. I knew where I wanted to be, but I wasn't convinced that I would actually reach that destination. Others labeled this as being negative. I preferred to think I was being realistic. After all, I am a realist.

At times, I avoided circumstances when I knew the social idiot complex would be too concentrated and too much for me to bear. Most times, I felt as though I resembled the childhood inflatable punching bag that would bop right back up whenever it was hit. I could be resilient or a glutton for punishment. Refusing the latter, I chose the defensive/ protective mode.

I intentionally refrained from situations that I knew would prove too difficult for me. After all, I had learned my limits by now. For example, the time had come to become employed again. However, my scope of interest had included only the jobs that I could complete from the comfort and safety of my own home.

I knew working in a professional environment would bring even more scrutiny to my already self-conscious persona. My differences would be highlighted. The inabilities I had tried so desperately to hide would now be so obvious. This included typing like a woodpecker. Once I had typed eighty words per minute. Now, the one-finger keyboard pecking would be quite apparent. My inability to use my left hand had severely minimized my ability to multitask. After all, my right hand could not simply split in half and do all simultaneously.

The Ripple Effect

Spouses

This is a position I do not envy as it carries a tremendous weight. I can only offer you encouragement as I did not exactly foster this for my husband.

If your spouse seems short-tempered or angry with you, he or she probably is. For that, I am sorry, but understand you are not the cause of the anger. You are simply the closest person. Unfortunately, you are the one who catches the brunt of your spouse's feelings. This can be brought on by the frustration and the unknown of the situation.

As the spouse, or close loved one, it is very important that both of you seek out individual counseling. Only a professional counselor can help by navigating both of you through the recovery process. During this winding road, I also suggest seeing a couple's therapist. Both partners may have mixed and overwhelming feelings of anger, disappointment, rage, depression, sadness, and grief. All of these feelings are completely understandable and justified.

A neutral third party can be a real blessing. This individual can convey to the partners exactly what the other is trying to say and convey to their partner. I also encourage that the two of you designate a time to talk about specific feelings so this does not consume every aspect of your time together.

I admit that I was not good at this. I voiced my frustration and sadness whenever I felt it. Not only did this wear my husband down, but I failed to recognize the pain and grief that both of us felt. I could only see the blazing bonfire of my own pain that was fueled by my everyday frustrations and inadequacies.

During this winding road, couple's therapy can be very beneficial because sometimes the distance that grows between two people is caused by missing one another. The couple may be speaking at each other, but they are not really conversing. Think of it as "speaking" sign language as you pass one another on the autobahn. The speed of flying emotions is virtually impossible to grasp.

Matters of the heart can be very difficult to navigate, especially when the tools were not in place before a tragedy. What better time to learn then when you can put them into practice. Believe it or not, both of you may share a major commonality: *fear.*

Both of you may wonder what the future holds. Ability or disability? Counseling is important because both partners need to have healthy outlets that are not directed at one another. Also, as the spouse and most likely the primary caretaker or support- giver, you need to have your "tank" filled so you are able to outpour love on your loved one. You can't run on empty and expect to hold it all together while maintaining a healthy relationship.

Again, this is based on what I did *not* practice. Therefore, it makes perfect sense, and now I can see its importance. I know that I wore my husband down when I would lash out from my mounting anger and frustration. Most specifically, I was frustrated with the continued lack of function in my left hand and arm.

Also, I would encourage the caretaker to go out with friends. It's important for the caretaker to have support as well as some normalcy and breathing room. These friends can help and hold you up in times when you may feel overburdened. I do suggest that those times be spent with healthy recreation as substance abuse could be attractive to drown out the pain and anger.

Another taboo area to be acknowledged is the intimate arena. Do not be surprised if these encounters are much less frequent. Most likely, the patient does not feel attractive. Physically, the patient's flexibility and maneuverability may not be as smooth as previously. Be patient during this process. Regardless of your loved one's present state and functionality, it is important to let your partner know how much they mean to you. So, continue to show you still adore your loved one.

I really struggled with this because I didn't feel as worthy and thought my husband loved me less because I was "broken". Totally absurd, but this was my heart's condition.

What can a couple learn? Take any horrific experience as an opportunity to really work on and establish a deeper relationship. The depth can come from finding the real meaning of the two of you, and your identity and meaning to each other.

Being benched absolutely sucks, but it can also provide an opportunity for growth and maturation. Date again. Set aside that one-on-one time that initially drew you close. Get the butterflies back in the pit of your stomach. The butterflies can have a tremendous healing benefit.

Children

Another area that is very important is the children, if you have them. Try to maintain some sense of normalcy. Make sure your children have friends and playdates to ensure a healthy escape from the tragedy as well. It is also important to consider talk therapy for the children as well.

I noticed a tremendous increase in my children's anger once they realized mommy was stuck this way for now. Their anger manifested in many ways. my children had more bouts of fighting back and screaming at me.

The level of respect for mommy in comparison to daddy's level of respect decreased amazingly. (Yes, kids most always seem to have more revere and respect for daddy than mommy.) However, it was exacerbated as the extent and frustration of my injury became more and more apparent. Naturally, this can add to the anger and frustration of the patient and spouse/partner.

One healing method, we used was to gather as a family to voice our feelings and anger. During this time, we passed around a pillow and a wooden spoon to beat the pillow. No holds barred on our feelings! We would all take turns hitting the pillow screaming at stroke.

I would also encourage establishing a routine and designated family time. We instituted Friday as a pizza and movie night. This was something that the kids could grasp onto every week. We also gathered together every night and watched a cake decorating show before the kids went to bed. Yes, it was a good show, but again, it was more about gathering and sharing our time and experiences. Not to mention it, the light hearted and happy show added much needed joy to our darkness.

Signs and Wonders

During this long winding road, I constantly prayed for signs of confirmation of God's presence and healing to come. The most common requested sign I prayed for was a rainbow. They appeared at the most random times.

One time, while driving from physical therapy to acupuncture, I began to sob. I called my mom and told her that I just wanted to die. My mom, scared for me, left work early to pick me up at therapy and drive me to my next appointment I had silently asked for a rainbow and told my mom of my prayer to see a rainbow. At that moment, she said, "Look!" as we sat at a traffic light.

I looked at the dirt encrusted car in front of us. A rainbow was drawn into the depths of dirt on the back windshield. An arrow pointed to it and the word rainbow was smeared into the dirt under the arrow. It screamed to me, *Here's your rainbow and it's spelled out for you so you don't miss it!*

To this day, that moment makes me smile. I really think God has a sense of humor and brings some light to an awful situation. From that moment, I saw rainbows at the oddest times. Even my children were excited whenever they saw one and were sure to point it out to me.

My therapists took to the hunt and prayed for their own confirmations. One even prayed for a rainbow as confirmation that I would get full use of my hand. Later, he told me that when he walked down a hallway with his son a rainbow appeared and spanned over the crest of a doorway. I heard many stories of rainbows that appeared for friends and family.

I also llistened for specific songs on my favorite radio stations. One song was introduced to me by a phlebotomist. I had gone for blood work and began to cry in the chair as I could no longer hold out my left arm to give blood. The kind spirited man told me about the song "Overcomer" by Mandisa. He then told me I would be an overcomer. He quickly became my angel.

As God's humor would have it, that song was one of the first songs I heard when I got in my car. I grasped at any sign I could get because my jaded blue eyes could see no hope anywhere. I also begged those around me to pray. Ask others to help hold up your arms when you are exhausted in prayer.

Prayer keeps us in sync with God. Prayer is the gas in the engine of our hearts and souls. Prayer develops a dependency on God. Humanity struggles with dependency on God because it does not feel natural or innate. By proclaiming, "I can't do it," we are not relying on God but rather our own strength. I quickly realized that I had faith for the world and others, but not for myself

Truth be told, I did not have the strength for this journey. Literally, this supernatural dependency was the only thing holding me up at times. Please understand, this is far too easy to recognize in hindsight. It is not as easy during a storm when waves crash and sharks circle in anticipation of their next meal. Drooling, they waited to devour me. Don't pray for god's sake, but for your own sake.

Believe me when I say that I had some serious struggles with my faith during this journey. I had questions that would never be answered. Those questions haunted me each day: Why did God let this happen? Why bless me with the life I have always wanted and then place me on the sidelines? Why let me watch the life I had helped to build go on without my participation? Why give me the strong desire for more children just to withhold my ability to carry them out?

My faith had been flipped, twisted, and turned inside out. I was no closer to getting any insight or relief. All I knew was that every time I had wanted to walk away from God, there was a strong tug in my heart that told me I shouldn't. Sometimes, the only one I could turn to was God.

Yet, He was the very object of my disdain and anger. When the therapy was getting me nowhere, I felt God was the only one who could help me. I was at the end of my limits. I was doing all that I could and needed another source to get involved. Along with this came insurmountable anger, and the feeling as though God was doing nothing about my situation.

During those moments, I could not even speak to God. I had many moments when I told Him I hated him. Initially, I felt guilty, but I began to learn that this expression was okay and genuine. God could handle my human-sized emotions even though I felt I could not. During these moments, I reached out to my church.

Although I had hoped and begged for a miraculous healing, I was not the lucky recipient. Still, that does not mean that miracles don't happen or that prayer is not beneficial. Although it cannot be proven, I am convinced prayer played a large part in my unpredictable and non-typical recovery as well as the healing of my arm and hand that were deemed lifeless.

Accept This?

Numerous times, my loving circle tried to convince me to accept what had happened and where I was. However, there was absolutely no chance of that occurring!

While I was in counseling one day, the counselor asked once again, "What word could you use to replace the word "accept"?

"Tolerate" was the only word that came to mind. How could I tolerate this until hopefully it would go away one day? I am still working on this concept, but it is not an easy task! For me, tolerating it was going about my life and forcing myself to do my typical tasks. These may not be done smoothly or pretty, I might add, but I am doing them nonetheless. And yes, I would have some good cries from time to time, especially as situations presented themselves that were emotionally difficult. These would include holidays, parties, children's activities, and dates with my husband.

I was continuously haunted with the previous me and the fear of what my future might look like. The current me stared back in the mirror. In a battle of wills, who would prevail? Me or the stroke? I was damned if I was going to let this new me stick around. I refused to accept.

This may have been one of the very things that made my journey that much harder. It led to some very dark days in which I wished I had died on the table. After all, what thirty-five year old wants to live out her days stuck like this? It could always be worse, but quite honestly, this was my "worse," and I could not imagine anything harder. Not only did I wish that I had died, but I hoped I would die now to end my suffering. This is where the anti-depressants really helped me pull up my big girl panties and press on.

I wish I had some largely impactful insight and words of wisdom to see the light and hold on. But quite honestly, the old Nike slogan, "Just Do It" is the only thing that comes to mind. Sometimes, it's just simply all you can do.

Unfortunately, there are no magic formulas or catch phrases. There are no twelve steps to this type of complex healing. It encompasses the physical, emotional and mental, aspects of our being. This is no easy feat. As everyone is different, the process is different for everyone. Therefore, individual healing cannot be placed in a box! Don't get comfortable on the bench, put your uniform back on piece by piece. Soon, you will be fully uniformed and ready to play your position.

Social Idiots

Those who try to regain normalcy in their lives will always encounter opposition. For me, this came in the form of ignorant people who never learned to keep their mouths' shut.

The Golden Rule states: "If you don't have anything nice to say, don't say anything at all." It seemed to apply only to children. The adults seemed to be ignorant of this courtesy or were never educated on etiquette. Therefore, they cannot help themselves from asking ridiculous questions. "What happened to you?" "What's wrong with your leg?" "Your walk is a little off."

Well, thanks for stating the obvious and telling me what I don't already know. Now, do they *really* want the truth or is it an excuse to be ignorant? "I had brain surgery, thanks for asking."

It came to the point where I wanted to make a T-shirt with: 1) brain tumor; 2) surgery; 3) stroke. The ignorance of others was especially difficult for me. I longed to be normal and worked really hard at pretending to be normal. I had always been a wall-flower so being thrust into scrutiny felt as though alcohol was being poured on an open wound

Being called out was a spear to my heart, especially when it happened in front of my children. It isn't easy to fight back tears while giving your children a lesson in compassion as well as what rudeness looks like and how our words can be a powerful weapon toward others. At one point, a store employee made a rude comment to me. My daughter began crying and told me, "Mommy, if I wouldn't get in trouble, I would run back in there and kick him!"

A generous offer, and yes, he did deserve that kick. But as a responsible mom caught in a teaching moment, I simply noted that some people are so ignorant and rude that a kick probably would do no good. I will have you know, after I had a chance to cool off, I did call the store management. I made it quite clear that their employees could use some training on customer respect and interaction. Thankfully, the management agreed and apologized profusely, stating that the said employee would be released. This was not the reason I called. I simply wanted to spare myself and others of the humiliation I endured. Another situation had happened one day when I was grocery shopping. Another mom had approached me with her son dtating that she could relate to my walk, I retorted that "No, I promise you that you cannot relate to my situation." She stated she thought I had knee surgery, but I proceeded to tell her why my walk was the way it was. It seemed to be a good 'open mouth, insert foot' moment for her and her child

As defined by Oxford University Press, compassion is: "sympathetic pity and concern for the sufferings or misfortunes of others". In other words, being sensitive and aware of how people are hurting around you.

Many people think that expressing compassion is done through acts of some sort or by making remarks. I beg to differ. Compassion can be expressed through a smile, by holding a door, or giving a small seed of kindness. When a production is made of someone's disability or comments are made, it actually defeats the entire concept of compassion.

Although others may think that they are offering compassionate comments, it often turns out to be plain ignorance. Nothing can be said to convey compassion in such a situation. The right thing can never be said. Sometimes, the lack of words speaks the loudest.

Unfortunately, mainstreaming may not be an easy task. But if you forge on, you will gain pride and self-respect as well as a sense of accomplishment. TBI doesn't win, You Do!

It's important to claim those victories when you can, no matter how small you think it is. Do this for you and your loved ones! This may mean using different ways to get things done. For example, use a pizza cutter to cut up waffles or other food. I woulduse a tray or bags to help carry multiple items to a different area. I would also hold spaghetti sauce jars between my knees to twist them open. I hated doing things differently than I had, but I would still get it done!

Boils Down to This

The moral of the story is *fight*. Fight with everything you have and for everything you want. Refuse to be benched. Force your way into the game. It may not be pretty or the way you'd like it to be, but do it anyway and feel pride in yourself for doing it.

Through this process, you will learn so much about yourself, how strong you really are, how resilient you are, and who you really are. Most likely, you will have moments of frustration and anger, but don't give up. The lighthouse will be within view! You may also learn something about your relationships. Which ones are genuine and will go the distance? Which ones are simply superficial and lack depth?

Unfortunately, it took trauma to test the endurance of my relationships with those close to me. Those which I thought had depth seemed to be the ones that made the deepest cut when they faded away as they claimed my problem was too big for them. Well, isn't that nice to have the luxury of walking away. I simply was not privy to that luxury.

Fortunately, my soul mate ran the distance with me, andfor that I am eternally grateful. This very dark and scary time not only brought us closer together, but it tested us more than most couples are tested during their entire lifetime. We took this time to learn more about ourselves and us.

Mind you, a lot of learning came from the groans of despair and the flow of tears that seemed to soothe us to sleep many nights. These were lessons I never wanted to learn, especially like this. But unfortunately, we don't always get to choose our hand of cards! The verse I wake to every morning that keeps me fueled is: *"Surely I will see the goodness of the Lord in the land of the living"* (Psalms 27:13 NIV). Framed on my nightstand, it is a daily reminder that if I put in the good fight I will see the glory of the Lord.

Mind you, there were many, many days in which I was not confident in seeing that glory! I constantly needed encouragement and hope from my friends, family members, my Stephen's mentor, and my chiropractic-neurologist. I am sure they were tired of my tears and doubts. I simply could not believe better and fully functioning days were ahead. I consider myself a realistic person. By telling myself that all would be well, I felt as though I was lying to myself since I did not know if this was really true.

I wish there was a magical answer or recipe to follow to make this journey easier and quicker. But the truth is that everyone is different and everyone's journey will be different. The rate of healing will be different, and the mindset of each individual will be different. Therefore, the coping methods and ability of each person will differ.

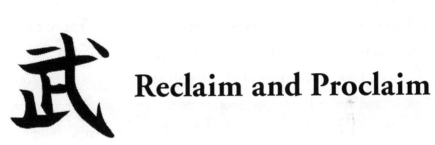

Reclaim and Proclaim

During the healing process, there is a point at which it is vital to reclaim as much of the "old you" as possible. This includes everything from your fashion as well as your social and romantic relationships. No, it will not be the same, but it is crucial in feeling more like yourself.

For me, this was dying a strand of my blonde hair purple. Why? To me, this was liberating. It allowed me to express the individuality I once held so dear. My individuality was clearly different now and needed to be redefined, so I felt as though I was healing and getting somewhere. I was also rewarding myself for the hell I had endured and the accomplishments thus far.

Did I get some looks from others? I sure did. However, I would much rather get looks for having purple hair, which was done by my choice, than for walking differently! I was proclaiming to the world, "Go ahead and look! I am a warrior!." I have also promised myself that when the use of my left hand returns, I will have the Chinese symbol for "warrior" tattooed on my left foot. This would be a symbol of meaning and conquering. I hope that day comes. Passersby wouldn't know what they were looking at, nor would they know my situation. But I would know, and that was what mattered to me.

During this time of proclamation, I took time to invest in others and my community by running for my local board of education and by playing a volunteer role in my local church's event called "A Night to Shine," created by the Tim Tebow Foundation. This was a prom for individuals with physical and mental disabilities.

Who better to advocate than someone who was walking in the shoes of the disabled. I had a chance to use my passion and conviction to help individuals with disabilities and personally advocate for them and their right to a night of normalcy and belonging. Now I had a taste of what these individuals experience on a daily basis with little hope of his or her disability being healed.

This was a conviction of mine to spread awareness of disabilities and TBI incidents. I also wanted to shed light on the feelings and mindset of disabled individuals. I did this by getting involved and giving back, I finally felt I was doing more than just living stroke. I had reestablished some value even though I still desperately desired complete healing and function.

Truth be told, many professionals seemed hopeful in my case. However, I had a difficult time feeling positive because this was the reality I woke to every day. That never seemed to change. I felt as though I had fast forwarded my life living my eighties in my thirties. Although time did relieve some of the shock of the situation, I experienced continuous grieving as every season and situation seemed to shed more and more light on my inadequacies and lack of ability.

For example, Christmas presented challenges in wrapping presents and carrying multiple packages as this elf had always done. Winter brought snow, which brought the desire of my kids to play in the snow and go sledding. I could hardly get my four-year-old dressed, As I could not zip her coat or put her mittens on. Yes, this situation had fostered some independence in my children, but I was also robbed of my "mommy-duty". Snow also brought sledding, which was hard for me. I could not climb up hills in the snow. Even if I did make it up, I couldn't hold onto the sled with two hands.

Defeat was a continuous battle. This injury was not something I could just sit down, mourn one time, and be over it as others had thought and so generously encouraged me to do. Continuous reminders and situations screamed, "This is real and still here!"

Finally, I had to look beyond the now and dream about what I would do when this was all over. I started to compile a list of dreams and celebrations I would partake in once my story had unfolded. This had included dreams of going on a cruise with my family. After all, we deserved an epic celebration. We needed to escape from this journey and reunite as a family within a joyous and fun context. I also decided to hold a healing party to celebrate with my therapists, friends, and family. I also looked forward to possibly pursuing my dream of adopting a child. After all, I was still a good mom and loved being one.

Lab Coat Lingo

When I had my first appointment with the chiropractic-neurologist, I had never even heard of such a profession. Shortly after my one-year anniversary of the TBI, I was walking without a cane. However, I was swinging my leg in a large circle (circumduction) to clear my foot to step forward. I did this because I had what was referred to as drop-foot. This meant I could not pull my foot up when I stepped forward, which resulted in tripping on my toes. It was a very annoying habit, and one I could not seem to break.

Most professionals just suggested I wear a foot brace. Quite simply, that was not going to happen. I refused because I was going to walk without anything. I also had a really hard time bending my knee to pull a step forward.

My chiropractic-neurologist assessed me on my first visit for over three hours. He spent a majority of the time assessing my eye movements and my VORs (visual ocular response). I had very unequal pupils. My left pupil was much larger than my right pupil.

After this initial visit, my doctor theorized that my brain thought I was spinning to the right, therefore contracting my left side. This caused me to constantly lean to the right. He also explained that I was most likely struggling with my left side because I was missing partial vision on my left side. He explained that my inability to move was a perception. My brain had a hard time recognizing the left side of my body and world.

He had given me many exercises to do, which I thought were completely crazy to break this involuntary thinking and retrain my brain. As crazy as they were, the exercises seemed to work! As time passed, I found my left side to be looser. Therefore, I no longer needed Baclofen, a drug prescribed to reduce the tone (or tightness on my left side). It was also, no longer thought I needed Botox injections, which yet another treatment option used to, reduce tone. These were victories! Stroke was not going to win!

So as crazy as my tasks and exercises were, they were working and I was advancing. I was also able to reduce, and almost completely overcome, the Clonis in my leg. This is a neurological side effect of a brain injury that causes the uncontrollable shaking of limbs. My left leg vibrated like crazy when I stepped down hard or moved it quickly. However, this diminished with my out-of-the-box approach of using chiropractic neurology.

I also had a condition typical to those with a brain injury. Which was that my left big toe was constantly erected and lifted up. This made walking very uncomfortable and putting slacks on very challenging. Once again, I was able to overcome and basically rid this condition. My left vision slowly returned, and my left arm began to hang straight when I stood at rest or walked. I was beginning to look and feel less and less of an orangutan. As time progressed, I was given more crazy tasks to complete that included many visual exercises.

While I remained diligent in performing these exercises, I noticed some changes although immediate function did not occur. I was informed that these changes would, in fact, lead to function. At one point, when I would sit down at night, my left hand and fingers would twitch like crazy. At that moment, I realized something must be happening because this had never occurred before. Granted, twitching was not function. But I kept hoping someday it would be. As time progressed, my VORs did start to normalize and equal out. My left pupil began to resemble the same size as my right pupil. My smile became equal and more symmetrical.

Allow me to offer some scientific insight per my chiropractic-neurologist. He was the one I constantly ran to in my moments of hopelessness. Two years is a long time to hold onto the hope that I would be normal again.

I encourage you with some neurological insight as per Dr. Vincent G. Kiechlin, DC, DACNB. When I asked for insight, he explained that when it comes to the brain you're never stuck with what you have. Such a statement can be made due to neuroplasticity,

Amazingly, neuroplasticity is the brain's ability to change due to changes in its environment. Nerve cells, like all cells in our body, have a cell membrane that surrounds the cell and holds all the parts inside. However, nerve cells are different from other cells. These cells have receptors that look like little arms that project off the membranes on the surface of the cell. These arms receive and transmit information to other cells in the nervous system. Every time a nerve cell does that successfully, that cell and all the other cells it communicated with become physically stronger. This physical change occurs in the brain when we learn.

Our brain performs this pruning and strengthening process throughout our entire lives. When the brain is injured, it immediately and automatically begins to repair the damage. It does so by pruning away the connections that can no longer be used by the brain; these are the cells that were damaged by the injury. The healthy brain cells around the injury immediately begin to form new connections where the old ones were pruned in an attempt to restore the lost function.

This process occurs even if the new connections are formed by cells that never had to perform that particular function in the past. New friendships and relationships are made to get the job done. This process can occur within hours, days, weeks, or months and years. Of course, all of the repairs are dependent upon the severity of the injury, the health of the brain prior to the injury, and the type and amount of stimulation coming into that area of the brain following the injury. Basically, the brain immediately begins to clean house and the damaged area begins to start over by making new friends and teams to get the job done.

These "acquaintances" among cells develop into lifelong friends to build a fully productive life and function. This is the exact point in the journey of my recovery, I am waiting for these pesky little neurons to shake hands and become acquainted. It's a very slow and frustrating process, one that could not go fast enough for me. After all, I had spent two years trying to forge these so-called friendships.

After working with the chiropractic-neurologist for over a year, he explained, in scientific words, that when I initially went to him I had a loss of voluntary motor function on the left side of my body. At the time, he felt some of this loss in function was due to the fact that I had lost peripheral vision to some areas of the left side of space.

Because of that visual disturbance, it is difficult for my brain to move into that area of space, which I no longer perceived visually. This includes movement of my spine, eyes, and limbs. As a consequence of this change, other systems in my brain that were not damaged, but associated with moving into that space, have decreased function as well. He believed that the loss of some of these systems, which were not damaged in my injury, is the result of a neuroplasticity change from my injury. The goal had always been to create neuroplasticity changes that are associated with normalization of those changed systems.

With this approach, my function has improved. However, it is nowhere near where I'd like it to be. Allow me to offer you proof of my visual improvement.

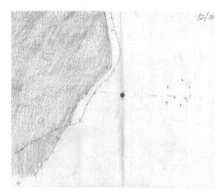 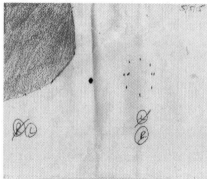

This was my initial blind spot test conducted by my chiropractic-neurologist on December 30, 2014. As you can see, I had a significant blind spot on my left side (the shaded portion). The dot in the middle represents the horizon. Initially, I could see nothing in this shaded area.

This image was from a subsequent test completed on May 5, 2015. After months of neurological exercises prescribed by my "out-of-the box," the left side had significantly improved.

The Choice Is Yours

After two years of fighting my way out of my situation, I attended church and was broadsided by my ignorance. The message that Sunday was about life throwing curve balls while you are stuck in a position you had never imagined.

Suddenly, the light bulb went on. We were taught that when we are in such terrible positions, we do have a choice. We can become bitter or use the circumstances to become a better person. Unfortunately, I had wasted the past two years in a puddle of bitterness. During that time, I didn't get anywhere. Instead, I had compounded the emotional pain I was feeling. Not only did I hurt myself, I hurt my family by not seizing the opportunity to grow and mature.

This does not mean that suddenly living with my disabilities was not going to bother me. I realized that I was doing myself no favors and needed to switch to become better through this challenge. I encourage a person who has experienced TBI to strive for better not bitter. Anything other than better is wasting your time and energy.

Once I decided to strive for better not bitter I used my voice and advocated for those who could not advocate for themselves. By doing my best, I gave insight about the TBI world and journey to others, especially, those professionals who have dedicated themselves to TBI treatment.

As the one living with TBI, choosing the path of bitterness makes this road much more difficult. Quite simply, TBI robs the joy from your life. I could not go back and change what had occurred. I could not make TBI magically go away. But I could make a choice each day to savor my accomplishments and time with my family. No, my life did not look how I had imagined, but the truth is I can't change it with the wave of a magic wand and a poof. Although God knows, I wish I could have! It all comes down to a choice. You can choose to be better or bitter. Yes, it is a choice. I implore you to choose better as bitter only compounds the pain and recovery process.

Choosing to be better does not mean I pranced around singing lalala. Because I was *angry*! And I had every right to be, but I had to make the choice to not let it consume me. This was not an easy choice to make or execute.

May this unfortunate journey mature you in unacknowledged ways and broaden your sphere of compassion and love toward others. It's a wonderful opportunity to learn true compassion. Please, do not mistake me thinking this situation is wonderful because I promise you it is not. However, it is a positive opportunity to stretch and mature in areas that you never knew possible. You are a survivor and a well-seasoned one at that!

The Silver Lining

I wish I could tie up this book with a nice little bow, but unfortunately, I am going on three years since my trauma, and I am still so far from where I want to be. I walk, but noticeably different, and I still have no purposeful function in my left hand and arm. As you can imagine, it's been a very long road and every day that I wake to this reality, is one more day I am walking blindly across country, as illustrated previously. Yes, everyday life has gotten easier; more so because I am learning to tolerate this, not accept it. I obviously am not living my life as I had pictured it, but so goes life. You can plan a route, but almost always hit a detour or construction. Well, I have hit a detour and I am absolutely a work in progress. I guess you could say, I am under construction.

However, I want to tell you, if you have suffered a similar trauma, you are not alone, and life does go on, as hard as that may be to imagine, I could not have imagined this three years ago, at the onset on my journey. I even remember asking others if my life would go on, and I can tell you it does, simply because I am there. If possible, try to recognize the short moments of normalcy and joy you may experience. Every such moment is one step closer to the finish line. You are winning! Now granted, this may not be easy to do, but it can be done. It will require intentional discipline and effort. Another insight would be to LAUGH!! Quite honestly, I have not been able to experience those moments of belly busting laughter, the kind that resonates from deep down in your being, bringing tears to your eyes. I had not laughed like that for years. However, I can tell I am healing on the inside as these moments are more and more.

Furthermore, savor your moments with your loved ones. Even if you may feel less than useful to them, honestly, they are just happy to have you around. Could you imagine the daily pain and torment they would experience if you had not made it. Whether you feel useful or not, you are present. In those dark moments picture your loved one's smile and envision their tears if your story had turned out any other way. Yes, you may shed tears, but they are not eternal, as your internal healing takes place, they do become less. I wish I could tell you, I don't cry anymore, but this is simply not true. There are still moments that prove too much for me to bear, serving me a reminder that I am limited in my abilities. If you are the loved one of one who has suffered a trauma, please be patient with these tears. They are simply healing ointment assuaging a deep wound. In other words, they may be necessary for emotional healing to occur. Although life may be different than you pictured, you can still make the best of it and hold your head up high, after all, you are tackling one of life's most difficult challenges, and for this you should be proud of yourself, you are marching on in the face of adversity. Not everyone can say they have done this but you are! Take a deep breath and "Just Do It." I believe you can and so do those around them, and if there are some that don't believe you can, prove them wrong, and not out of spite, but rather self-confidence!

Another highly insightful piece of advice I would suggest is to "fake it until you make it." Sometimes it helps to force yourself to smile. Sometimes this can feel like you are taking sandpaper to your face, but 'holding it together' can sometimes just simply mean tightening the girdle on your emotions and spitting in the face of adversity by smiling through the pain. No, not the afore mentioned perma-grin, but rather a sincere gesture of grasping the joy in life because even though you may not feel it, it does exist

A letter to the caregivers and or loved one on behalf of the trauma survivor

I know this is not the life we imagined but I am glad you are the one walking this unchartered road with me, and maybe now you are the hands that are pushing me forward but please know how grateful I am for those hands and for the smiles we share gliding my wheels over the rough and unpredictable terrain. Thank you also for the care you provide for me in the moments of my indecency. Thank you for maintaining my humanity and dignity in those less than flattering moments. Let's make memories of our shared fumbles in those times of awkwardness. Inside jokes that only you and I will understand, forming and sharing a common ground of tolerance as we mock life's attempt to knock us to the ground. Laughing may provide us the internal healing we so desperately crave. Thank you for all of the sacrifices you have made to care for me the best, and for thinking of me first and foremost. Although I may not express my gratitude to you as often as I should, please know though I may not verbalize it, please hear it through my smile, my eyes, my touch. The gratitude and appreciation is there and is being expressed, maybe just in a way you are not accustomed to hearing or experiencing

Gratefully,
Your loved one

A letter to the trauma survivor,

Take heart my friend...you can and will get back up and play on the team, whether this is physically, mentally or emotionally. Where you are now is not where you will stay. This is just a chapter in your book; it's not the whole book. Although this may feel like the end, it's actually a beautiful beginning of a new wiser, stronger and a more mature you. You have just learned one of life's most treasured lessons: take nothing for granted. What seemed like problems before are now just trivial hiccups in our existence. Unfortunately not everyone has a chance to learn this lesson and now you have perspective, my friend, a broken nail or coffee stain on a white blouse is now just a frivolous happenstance. You can now appreciate the ease of life and can provide your own insight to those who may be caught up in the pettiness of everyday life. I encourage you to hold your head up high. And take a breath of confidence and accomplishment. Everyday you face the day head on is an accomplishment. Stay proud and determined

With utmost sincerity,
Your sister in circumstance

Printed in the United States
By Bookmasters